home & hope

Noor Afasa

BookLeaf Publishing

India | USA | UK

Presentation by *BookLeaf Publishing*

Web: www.bookleafpub.com

E-mail: info@bookleafpub.com

ISBN: 9789358315530

First edition 2023

To those who make life better,

I appreciate you.

I pray you are always happy and healthy

Ameen

ACKNOWLEDGEMENT

Thank you to everyone who has come into my life, bringing even the slightest bit of happiness.

Family and friends, thank you for endlessly giving me your love and support. You are always in my duas.

I want to thank Mariyah, Saoirse and Evie AGAIN for being my inspiration and helping me become the confident, young woman I am today.

And Ammi, I could not thank you enough for all you do. I am beyond proud to call you my mum - I love you.

PREFACE

I began to write poetry during the first covid lockdown and to be honest, I can't remember what exactly had pushed me to pick up a pen, put it to paper and start writing but I am glad that I did. Overtime, I believe that I have improved through the help I have been given by others and their honest feedback. I have also improved through getting involved in competitions, projects and so on. Poetry is a passion of mine and I will always work towards improving to make use of the power my words can hold.
So, thank you for purchasing and choosing to read this (my second book!!) -
it means a lot.

In this book, I have attempted to explore and write about two things that up until recently, I have always been reluctant on discussing openly and being expressive about: my culture and my religion. I wanted to create a collection of poems similar to the what I wish I could see more of in books. I hope you find yourself relating to some of my poems and enjoy your read!

comfort in tea

in my culture nobody asks if you are okay
if everything is alright
but instead, ask 'chaa peeso?'
no sweet, comforting words
just two teaspoons of sugar
no warm, comforting hugs
just two hands hugging a hot teacup
simple sweet sips
replace salty tears

it's not about how much milk to add,
but about the person you're making it for.
it's not about the biscuits to give with it,
but what you can say to make them feel better.
for us, the offering of tea is how we ask
'are you okay?'
and when we sit together, it means
'i am here for you.'

pakistani

i am the difference between pothwari and
punjabi
the difference between 'menu' and 'mikki'
i am the spices in my mother's sabzi
the jingle-jangle of my golden anklets
- noisy but magical.

i am the mehndi that stains your hands -
the intricate designs spread across your palms
i am the roundness of your rotis
sequins on your shalwar kameez
- irritating but beautiful.

i am the beats of a dhol
the vibrancy of colours dancing and twirling
around your scarf
i am the mithai eaten at a relative's house
i am multiple cups of chaa
- unhealthy but sweet.

i am your local bazaar
i am the tikka on your forehead
the decision between 'white... or traditional red?'
i am practised dance steps.

i am meeting you with a handshake and two
pecks
i am saying goodbye - about another fifty times
i am the difference between pothwari and
punjabi
"tenu punjabi ni aunda?"
"na, may pothwari bolni ah."

alhamdulillah

no matter the sadness i feel
or the pain.
or the worries that haunt me everyday.
whatever burdens i am made to bear
you will not hear me complain
no need to ask if i am okay
because my reply will always be the same
"alhamdulillah"

i don't need a shoulder to cry on
or my tears to be wiped
don't need your hand to hold
nor someone to understand me
but,
once i am home
within the safety of my walls
i will lay out my prayer mat
inhale, and
raise my hands to my lord
allow my forehead to rest against the floor
exhale,
whisper "ya Allah'
and let my worries be no more.

dream

i once asked my mum about what she wanted to
be when she was younger,
what kind of life she hoped to lead,
the type of man she wanted to marry,
how she wanted to raise her children and
the home she planned to decorate.
i was surprised,
when she told me she had never thought about
any of this when she was little.
guilty,
because she is the reason i am able to dream
today
and the reason that they become reality.

if i could write to the little girl who grew up and
is now my mum
the letter wouldn't be that long
i know what i would write,
if i could meet and tell her anything
i know what i would say
i would tell her one thing,
to dream.

eid mubarak

it's repetitive, the same each and every year
yet it always feels more magical than the last
one.

nothing more beautiful than dhikr
altogether as a family
"Allahu akbar"
(God is the greatest)
our voices intertwine into one
in remembrance of our lord -
a remedy for the soul.

the best part is giving salaam
greeting everyone as they arrive
handshakes and kisses
compliments and hugs
selfies and wishes

then we all start bringing in the food
sometimes sneaking a bite beforehand
running down to sneak a samosa or kebab
we all sit together
chatter, laughter and duas
so much happiness in gifting money,
knowing God will reward you so much more

then we start at the first relative's house
sometimes too tired
too full
to visit another and
so leave it to the next day
but there is no better feeling
than the one when we say
"eid mubarak"

our natural home

you may not understand
why we stop to feel
the heat of the sun caress our faces,
except that it feels natural.
or why it satisfies our soul
to have the wind blow in our hair
and the leaves whisper in our ears,
except that it is all we truly know.

away from our 9 to 5s
repetitive lives
colleagues to meet
and no time to eat,

nature requires no skill.

home & hope

my home outside of home
is not a place
but can be found in the silence between
conversations
it can be felt in the warm embrace of others
in the cup of tea made by my mum
or hidden between the pages of a book
i feel at home
within these moments of hope.

a remedy for the soul

what cools and soothes,
what satisfies my soul is
dhikr.
sat in a dimly lit room with my muslim sisters
but soon as my eyes close
it feels as though it is just me and my Lord.

all worries are washed away
and any doubts are cleared,
my chest fills with warmth
as i whisper phrases of praise -
whispering a remedy for my soul.

a land of spices, samosas and sun

i wish to see the village my father grew up in,
the dusty roads he ran along
and the tight streets he rode through.
i wish to taste the sweet mangoes he grew in the
summer.

i wish to climb the trees my grandma climbed
and plucked sour berries from,
to collect grass, like she did,
in a home-made basket, carry it on my head to
feed the animals later.
i wish to meet my grandma's friends and listen to
the conversations she had as she carried water
back from the well in a clay pot.

i wish to run in the fields,
where my grandad tended to his sheep and
to experience the love he received from his
village friends.
i wish to feel his sadness
when he had to leave behind his home as a
sacrifice for his children.

i wish to know about their lives in a land that will always be their home.

flower garden

when compared to flowers,
it doesn't always mean fragility.

it's important to note
flowers aren't as fragile as we thought.
but that,
they stand tall
stubborn against strong winds,
and refusing to fall.
and don't forget their extraordinary beauty
as they bloom and grow
yes, we are flowers
beautiful and strong

a letter to myself

oh little girl,
do not feel ashamed.
do not feel any less and shy away.
be proud
but i know you aren't
and you will grow to regret it one day.
but, don't worry
it's okay
because you will grow up to love your skin
in an amazing way
your teabag-stained skin
rich and brown like soil
smooth as chocolate

oh little girl,
you will
grow up
and find that
your brownness is your beauty.

feeling

feeling is a strange thing.
and complicated
from hurt, to love and loneliness
feeling is a strange thing
but beautiful.
where we long to feel the touch of our loved
ones one last time
where we seek safety in the warm embrace of
another
relieved to have someone to share your worries
with,
where our tears can mean either
happiness or sadness.
feeling is a beautiful, strange thing.

the storytellers

deeply etched lines hug her lips
as though Happiness itself carved them there,
her lips remain unmoving and silent
yet, they tell me joyful stories of her life.

and his eyes
they glisten with tears
as though Sadness itself resides there,
his eyes remain unblinking and still
yet, reveal the endless hardships he has found
himself facing
and how all his life,
struggle is all he has known.

and my lips
they don't move,
i have nothing to say.
and my eyes are the same,
for i have no tears to cry.
and so my eyes imitate my lips -
they close.
for all i can do for these storytellers is
to listen.

false fairy tales

what is a fairy tale?
a delightful telling
of a shooting star
and secret lands
near and far.

and in love with his beloved princess,
maybe a chivalrous knight
but beware of the villainous witch -
she's a dreadful sight.

but growing older means
you learn
that shooting stars don't grant your wishes,
and secret lands are a myth,
a hopeless empty promise.
and that chivalrous knight isn't so brave after all,
it was a lie that we had been told.
he didn't save any princess
from a castle so tall.
no, that fairy tale was completely false
to cover his faults
make himself feel better,
and cast the princess away into the shadows.

being a woman, it will only take one written and
stamped letter.

and perhaps,
a similar tragedy befell the villainous witch;
it's possible that she had been a princess until
one day,
a day where her magical grown
lost it's magic
and left behind a miserable frown.
oh, what a wretched thing
a wretched being
for living alone
because after everyone had chosen to leave,
loneliness is the only comfort she had known.
what a wretched woman
…for feeling?
for being dismissed and broken,
"she doesn't belong here"
the people have spoken.

what is a fairytale?
growing older means
you learn
that a fairy tale
sometimes means
falsehood.

my piece of paradise

i once read a poem
that spoke of paradise.
it read, "and when we talk about paradise
I talk about my Mother" -
it made me think about my piece of paradise on
earth.
the strong woman i long to reunite with in
jannah,
whose body not only carried me, cared for me
but carries paradise beneath her soft footsteps.
the woman whose name translates to
'wild rose'.
and although there will be all types of bliss in
paradise
and any desires of flowers, food and fragrances
will be granted;
no matter the abundance of flowers in jannah,
i pray to meet my wild rose there.

miscarriage

sat in front of her,
silently ashamed - i have no comforting words
nor the want to hug her.
what could i give?
what use would it be
when all she's wanted has been taken
repeatedly?

her hand placed longingly on her stomach,
i bite my tongue.
i stay still.
the silence consuming - no disruption.
the silence is unhelpful
but that's what she needs.
a moment - to stay still and believe,
that her baby is still with her
and it's happiness she feels instead of grief.

she befriends pain in the most unusual way.
hungry and weak
sadly tracing her stretchmarks,
refusing to sleep.

pain is what gives her feeling
one broken heart and many pieces

a constant reminder,
of her baby in heaven;

the child she couldn't have
but, yet will love forever.

i am muslim

i am the adhan,
calling you to prayer
waking you up at dawn
to pray to your Lord -
the most beautiful reminder.
i am the whispered prayers
whilst the rest of the world is silent and still.
magical.

i am practised tajweed.
repeating line after line
just to get it right,
to be able to smile
hearing how lovely it sounds.
beautiful.

i am the water used to cleanse your arms
and pass over your head.
the panic to arrive at the mosque in time.
i am the sadaqah you give daily
to ensure one's happiness and safety.
rewarding.

i am the laid out prayer mat
for you to rest your forehead against,

to pour out your heart
and lighten your burdens.
relieving.

dream catcher

forget a dream catcher
tell me your dreams
so i can collect and keep them safe,
share them with you again.
remind you of your worth
make you feel whole again.

maternal love

the womb that expanded
and the body that bled,
if not a woman, who else could do that for you?
who else would do that for you?

identity

my bangles create laughter
as i rush about the house
everyone laughing with

my jhumke chatter
to each other
their secrets slipping into my ears

my anklets whisper
trying to keep quiet
shushing the others,
but i guess i am just proud with being pakistani -
i want to show everyone
and have everyone know.

www.ingramcontent.com/pod-product-compliance
Lightning Source LLC
La Vergne TN
LVHW041253200726
843507LV00013B/2938